A Guide to Edutainment Gaming II:

The Early Microcomputer Years

By Anthony "Gamer" Ventrello

This book is dedicated to Verl and JoAnna, of course; but also, my fellow teachers, both past and present, who keep edutainment gaming alive. And to my fellow gaming YouTubers: Kim Justice, Lady Decade, James Rolfe, John Hancock, and Metal Jesus Rocks; thank you for your assistance and your knowledge of old-school gaming. Without you all, this book wouldn't be possible.

In Memory of Daniel Leggitt and Jason Greer.

Introduction

In my previous book *A Guide to Edutainment Gaming*, I focused on the early console years. I discussed edutainment games for the first home consoles from the Magnavox Odyssey to the Atari 5200 and everything in between. My reason for writing that book was simple: I believe that edutainment games never go out of style. All other gaming genres do. I was just at Costco the other day and I saw a trailer for the new Madden game. I looked at the gameplay for a few seconds, turned to my wife and asked, "Isn't there such a thing as being too realistic?" I mean I remember a time when you had to use your imagination when you played games. Like on *Warlords*, where you imagined yourself as a king throwing lightning and fire balls at the three other kings, hoping that your shot will blast through their castle and end them. Of course, the sprites were squares and rectangles, but back then, imagining was half the fun!

I'd be curious to see what a modern adaptation of *Warlords* would be like. It would probably have cut scenes and explosions and all kinds of stuff. You know, the more I talk about it, the more I'd like to see it! But anyway, the point is that video games have changed drastically since the mid 70's.

One thing that hasn't changed is the necessity of education. And what is taught, for the most part, has remained unchanged. There are certain basic skills that EVERYONE must learn. And one of the best ways for young learners to do that is by edutainment gaming. As I showed in my last book, there are many old games that are still relevant today. And since emulators and vintage gaming consoles can be used, with a little tweaking, on modern TV's and computers, they can still be used today in both classrooms and at home.

In this book I'm going to discuss edutainment gaming on the first microcomputers. The 2016 Census tells us that 89% of US households have a computer.[1] This was a big shift from October of 1984 when only 8.2% of US household had one.[2] In the years before that, microcomputers were limited to businesses and schools, as they simply were too expensive for most middle-class consumers. After the Video Game Crash of 1983/84, software companies focused more on making both regular and edutainment games for computers. And as time went on, computers became more affordable, until they became a necessary part of each household.

The games I'm going to discuss in this text come from the early years of edutainment computer gaming: the late 70's to around 1990. I will use the same format as I did in my previous book: The game's title, description, educational focus, year of release, company, programmer, variations, and fun fact. As a teacher and a long-time gamer, myself, I have personally played and recommend each of the games listed in this book. I hope you enjoy it, and please do get in touch with me and let me know if I missed any.

Thanks!

Anthony Ventrello

Summer 2023

---

[1] https://www.census.gov/content/dam/Census/library/publications/2018/acs/ACS-39.pdf?#:~:text=In%202016%2C%20the%20American%20Community,common%20feature%20of%20everyday%20life.

[2] https://www.census.gov/history/pdf/computerusage1984.pdf

Contents

Apple II/e

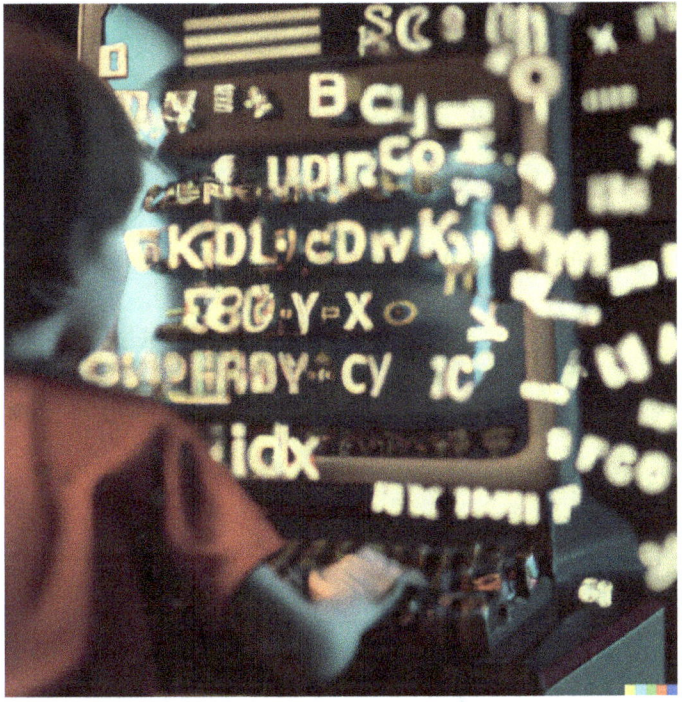

Like many students that grew up in the 80's, the Apple II/e was my first introduction to a

personal computer. I was one of the few students chosen to participate in a summer program

dedicated to computers. It was the summer after my 3rd grade year, and the year was 1984. We

went through the basics of BASIC, learning how to turn it on and off properly, Control, Open-

Apple, Reset and all that good stuff. It started what would become a lifelong love affair between

me and computers. I wanted to learn all that I could about them and have spent a good deal of

my time doing just that.

I have to say that Apple was smart in that they donated their computers to schools all over the

country. That really gave them a leg-up over their competitors. After a few years, every

classroom had at least one computer, whether the teachers knew how to use it or would let the

kids use it was another story. Still, thanks to Apple, microcomputing and education would go

hand in hand.

For the remainder of my school career, I would work with Apple II/e computers. In middle school we had to take three years of computer classes, 6 weeks each. I really enjoyed the classes and would have preferred to stay in them all year, instead of having to go back to PE. We learned how to type (well, some of us did), use Apple Works, Logo, and make our own newspaper using a program that I totally forgot about. Although the classes were both fun and informative, I have to say that the pacing wasn't good. Too much was expected of the students in the scant 6 weeks we had. I hope that in the coming years they either fix that or make the class year long. That's what I would have done, anyway.

During those years I was exposed to some amazing edutainment games. And they still hold up today, as edutainment games are just about the only genre of games that do not age out. I know that there are thousands of great edutainment games for the iconic Apple II/e computer, but I'm going to just discuss the ones that I, personally, utilized growing up. I'm sure that many of my readers, who are in the same age range as me, have also played many of the games that I'm going to discuss. As always, if you have some memories you'd like to share, please feel free to. And of course, if you don't happen to have an Apple II/e handy (I've seen them go for pretty reasonable prices on eBay and on the atariage forums), you can use an emulator. The best one that I have found is AppleWin. It works great and you will swear that you are actually back on that classic computer. You can get the program at this link:

https://github.com/AppleWin/AppleWin

So now let's go back to those good old days when there was not yet an Internet, discs were floppy, hard drives were not used for storage, most computers didn't have a mouse, and our computers were all one piece and weighed about as much as the family car.

MECC - Minnesota Educational Computing Consortium (later Corporation)

This game company, which was founded in 1971, was all about edutainment gaming. Initially their focus was making edutainment games for the schools in the state of Minnesota, but later they went on to service schools around the world. Their first big game was *Oregon Trail*, which we will be talking about in detail. As time went on, their library grew, and they made games for several different computer platforms besides the Apple II/e. Eventually they were acquired by Softkey in 1995 and shut down in 1999. But their legacy lives on through their games and the millions of children around the world that found out that learning can be fun.

Lemonade Stand

Description - A business simulation/text game that was originally created by Bob Jamison in 1973 and was later ported to the Apple II/e computer. The player starts their own lemonade stand and is given a set amount of money to spend on supplies and advertising. You will determine how many cups to sell each day and how much to charge. Your success will be determined by how much profit you make. Several factors can determine your sales such as weather, road construction and other things. Multiple players can compete against each other to see who can make the most money.

9

Educational Focus - Economics, Math, Problem Solving

Year of Release - Initially it was released in 1973 but was later ported to the Apple II/e computer in 1979.

Programmer - (1973) Bob Jamison & (1979) Charlie Kellner

Variations - One or more players

Fun Fact - For years this game was included with the purchase of an Apple II/e computer. It was also offered with a bundle of children's software for use with the Atari 8 computers.

Oh, Deer!

OH, DEER!

WHITETAIL HOLLOW

Description - *Oh, Deer!* is an educational simulation game where the player has to control the population of a deer herd around a suburban community. The aim is to reduce the size of the herd to a level that can be supported both by the land and the people. The game deals with wildlife population dynamics and management issues as well as how human-defined values are applied to animals in the environment.

The game is played over five years. At the start of each year, the player chooses one of seven actions from a menu. The actions that can be taken include removing deer by trapping or shooting, planting food in areas away from homes, spraying repellents on shrubs, scaring the deer away or to do some research. After choosing an action, statistics show the development of the herd during the year and how much it costs. A public approval rating is then given.3

Educational Focus - Ecology, Biology, Problem Solving, Economics

Year of Release - 1983

Company - MECC

Programmer - Philip Bouchard, Cynthia Schroader and Bob Granvin

Variations - Programs:

---

3 https://www.mobygames.com/game/136231/oh-deer/

- *White Tail Hollow*

- *Herd Management*

Other Options:

- *General Information*

- *End*

Fun Fact - I first played this game when I was in the Computer Club while in middle school. It was challenging back then, and still is!

Oregon Trail

Description - In this iconic game you take on the role of a pioneer that is traveling from Independence, Missouri to Oregon in a covered wagon, in the year 1848. You decide what your occupation is (this will determine how much money you have and how skilled you are with repairs, etc.), which supplies to purchase, when to leave for your trip, and many other decisions that can mean the difference between life and death. The goal is to make it to Oregon with as many members of your party as you can. There are some great mini games like hunting and rafting down the river. You will never play the same game twice, as every new game is an adventure!

Educational Focus - History, Problem Solving, Decision Making, Economics, Life Skills

Year of Release - The original version (now lost) was originally developed by Don Rawitsch, Bill Heinemann, and Paul Dillenberger in 1971. It was re-released over the years, but the most recognizable version was made for the Apple II/e computer in 1985.

Company - MECC

Programmer - John Krenz

Variations -

- *Travel the Trail*

- *Learn about the Trail*

- *See the Oregon Top 10*

- *Turn Sound Off*

Occupations:

- *A banker from Boston*

- *A carpenter from Ohio*

- *A farmer from Illinois*

Fun Fact - This game has been rereleased and rebooted over the years for different computers.

In recent years the Apple II/e version was released on a handheld device.

Bonus - Ways to Tell that You Play Too Much *Oregon Trail*

Let's face it, many of us that are now in our 40's and 50's have played this game more times than we can count. We try and try and don't quit until we can make it to Oregon with everyone in our party still alive and healthy, and with at least some cash. Even then we still keep trying to beat our last score.

So, for all of those who have died from Cholera, drown in a river, and have successfully repaired a wagon wheel in the middle of the desert, this one's for you:

- You go to the meat market and purchase 500 lbs. of beef, but only take 100 lbs. home with you.

- It takes you double the time to get to a vacation destination because you insist on stopping for a day at every historical landmark.

- You go on a hunting trip, and you can't understand why animals don't just walk up to you.

- When taking US History in high school the teacher asks, "What did Abraham Lincoln die from?" and you answer "Dysentery."

- If you've ever sunk your car in the river because you tried to caulk it and float it across.

- You get lost while on vacation and you offer a Native American man a set of clothes to guide you.

- When you hear the word 'yoke', breakfast isn't the first thing you think of.

- Your kids ask you to take them to Disney World, but you insist on going to Willamette Valley in Oregon.

- You see a headstone on the side of the road, and you check to see if it is someone from your US History class.

- You are convinced that 90% of the deaths in the 19th century were due to typhoid.

- You refuse to take a plane to any far-away destination.

- You got arrested for driving a covered wagon on the highway.

- Instead of buying apples at the store, you drive around town looking for apple trees to pick from.

- You have a stockpile of food and clothes in your car.

- You have more than one spare tire for your car.

- Your neighbor gets his car stuck in a ditch and you hire a team of oxen to pull him out.

- You actually own a team of oxen.

- You recognize pictures of the Green and Snake Rivers, even though you've never been to either.

- You are surprisingly happy and jovial when all members of your family make it to your vacation destination.

- You get the highest score in your class on *Oregon Trail,* and you strongly consider trail guide as a profession.

- You get lost in your neighborhood but could find your way to Idaho with your eyes closed.

- On a job application, where it asks for skills, you write that you successfully completed *the Oregon Trail* with all the members of your party.

- You get lost in the trails in the woods behind your house and it takes you a whole day to get home.

- You go hunting and are generally surprised that deer don't always drop where you shoot them.

- When asked which occupations you are considering for your future you list farmer, carpenter or banker.

- You refuse to leave on an extended family vacation until March.

- You insist your family have a sing-along to 19th century American songs.

- Instead of going to Branson, Missouri you go to Independence, Missouri.

- You win the lottery and your first task at hand is to recreate the *Oregon Trail* experience in real life.

- You try to finance a real-life *Oregon Trail* experience but are surprised when the prices for supplies aren't the same as in the game.

Sunburst Technology Corporation

This edutainment gaming company started in 1972. Many of the games that they are famous for were only available to schools and educators. When I started to seek out games that I played when I was younger, I had a hard time finding many of the titles that Sunburst made. I did eventually find them, but it wasn't easy.

Even though they have gone through different owners, mergers, and names, Sunburst is still around today. They are still enhancing learning for students around the world.

Memory Castle

Description - *Memory Castle* is an educational game where the player is a knight who has to enter and accomplish tasks in a castle. The game gives instructions to the player who has to memorize them. The player is then asked questions on what should be done next, for example where to go, and has to answer correctly to progress through the game. An incorrect answer leads to the game ending. 4

Educational Focus - Short Term Memory, Problem Solving, Color Identification, Following Directions

---

4 https://www.mobygames.com/game/82642/memory-castle/

Year of Release - 1983

Company - Sunburst Communications Inc. and Rochester School District

Programmer - Lon Koenig

Variations -

- Easy, Medium, & Difficult

Fun Fact - This was a favorite game for many when I was in elementary school. But that didn't mean many of us were good at it.

For Your NEXT Adventure

Description - You have just met a friendly robot which has escaped from the Robot Corporation. Because it contains Safety Circuits, this robot cannot hurt a human being. You learn from this robot that someone has created a bad robot without Safety Circuits, which can harm humans. You must help the friendly robot infiltrate Robot Corporation and find and fix the defective robot.

Through different levels, the player must move the robot by typing in X or Y coordinates and stating the current and desired location of the robot. The player must pick up, use, and drop items to solve puzzles.[5]

Educational Focus - Graphing, Geometry, Critical Thinking Skills

Year of Release - 1985

Company - Sunburst Communications Inc.

Programmer - Robert C. Rosen

Variations – 1 player

Fun Fact - Although this game was designed for children, adults also find it challenging.

---

[5] https://www.mobygames.com/game/188829/for-your-next-adventure/

Challenge Math

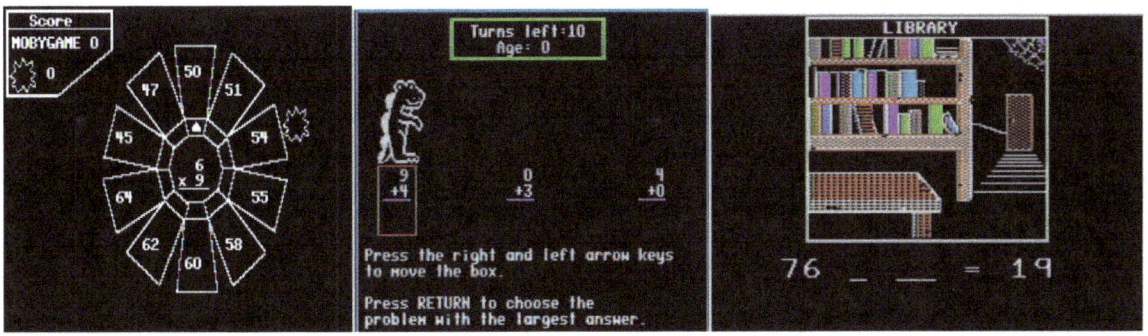

Description - *Challenge Math* is a series of 3 different math games for multiple systems:

In *Alien Intruder*, the player chooses whether to do addition, subtraction, multiplication, or division questions. Answers are arranged in a circle with 4 - 12 spokes depending on the player's choice. The player is given an equation in the center and must select the correct answer before the alien invader chooses it. If the player chooses incorrectly or is too slow, the spike is destroyed. If the player is correct, the spike is recovered. At the end of the game, the player and alien invader receive a score. In *Digitosaurus*, the player must choose which of three equations has the highest sum and direct the dinosaur to eat this equation by typing the correct answer. Every correct answer causes the dinosaur to age 55 years, with the dinosaur reaching 600 years of age if all 10 questions are answered correctly. In *Math Mansion*, the player moves about different rooms of a house collecting items to escape. Every move or picking up an item requires the player to successfully fill in the numbers to complete a mathematical equation. The player must gather a sword, candle, rope, and sledgehammer. These items can then be used to escape from the mansion to freedom.6

Educational Focus - Math: Order of Operations, Basic Math

Year of Release - 1982

Company - Sunburst Communications, Inc.

---

6 https://www.mobygames.com/game/143689/challenge-math/

Programmer - C. McMahon & J. Sweedler

Variations –

- *Alien Intruder* - Addition, Subtraction, Multiplication and Division.

- *Digitosaurus* - 3 different skill levels

- *Math Mansion* – 1 skill level

Fun Fact - When I was in 4th grade, our teacher would allow us to play these games when we got our regular work completed. We used to laugh when the dinosaur appeared to fart on the numbers.

Broderbund

One of the most memorable computer-related companies from the 80's had to be Broderbund. Why? Those were the guys who made *The Print Shop*, of course. I can't tell you how many millions of gallons of ink were used on those dot-matrix printers to make signs, cards, and occasionally banners. Nothing said I love you more than a card that you made on *Print Shop*. Besides that, Broderbund was also known for making both regular and edutainment games. Sadly, Broderbund was no more as of 1998, but its many products and programs are still around for modern computers. For those of us that grew up during its heyday, there was no one better for both entertainment and edutainment than Broderbund.

Carmen Sandiego Franchise

Starting back in 1985, Broderbund released a game called *Where in the World is Carmen Sandiego?*, and that started the whole franchise which has branched out into several games, tv shows, cartoons, a game show, and other things. The premise of the series is that you are a detective from an agency called ACME and you are trying to track down members of a gang called V.I.L.E. and arrest them. You travel to different places around the world, country, space, etc., collecting clues in order to obtain a warrant from Interpol so you can arrest the thief who has stolen some great treasure. Your ultimate goal is to nab the leader of V.I.L.E. herself, Carmen Sandiego.

There were several games in the series that have been ported to several different platforms and have been updated as time has gone on. HarperCollins now owns the rights to the franchise, and of this writing, the latest game *Where on Google Earth is Carmen Sandiego?* was released in 2019 (you can still play it online). Let's hope they keep making Carmen games for each new generation of students.

Where in the World Is Carmen Sandiego?

Description – In this game you take on the role of a detective from ACME (you get to pick your name) and you are in pursuit of some thieves from a group called V.I.L.E. (they never said what that stood for). Some thieves would steal some items of historical value from a city and you had to obtain clues, follow them, obtain an arrest warrant from Interpol, and ultimately arrest them in a set amount of time. You had to utilize your skills in both geography and history in order to utilize the clues given to track down the thieves. As time goes on, you receive promotions, the assignments get harder, and your ultimate goal is to arrest the queen of thieves herself: Carmen Sandiego

Author's Note – The versions from both the 80's and 90's are outdated as the names of countries and currencies have changed since then. Example – The Soviet Union no longer exists and several countries in Europe now use The Euro as their currency. With that in mind, at this point this version of the game is only practical to someone who was around back then. Students can still use the game to learn about history, but much of the data in the game is not current.

Educational Focus – History, Geography, Current Events

Year of Release – 1985

Company – Broderbund

Programmer - Dane Bigham

Variations – 1 player

Fun Fact – When you purchased this game, *The World Almanac and Book of Facts* was packaged with it.

Where in the USA is Carmen Sandiego?

Description – In this sequel to *World,* you are once again an ACME detective on the trail of Carmen and her henchmen. This time they are stealing treasures from major US cities, and you have to track them all across the country. Your knowledge of both US History and Geography will help you to follow the thieves, understand clues, obtain an arrest warrant, and finally arrest them and return the stolen property to its rightful owners.

Education Focus – US History, Geography, States & Capitols

Year of Release – 1986

Company – Broderbund

Programmer - Glenn Axworthy

Variations – 1 Player

Fun Fact – When you purchased this game it came with *Fodor's USA Travel Guide.*

Where in Europe is Carmen Sandiego?

Description – In this 3rd game in the Carmen Sandiego franchise, you chase Carmen and her henchmen across 34 European countries. Of all the games, this one is the most difficult as a real knowledge of European and World History is a must in order to be successful.

Author's Note – This game was released in 1989, therefore the state of Europe has changed since then. Some countries that were around then are no longer in existence and much of Europe now uses the Euro instead of their local currency. A newer version of this hasn't been released as of this writing.

Educational Focus – Geography, World History, European/Western Civilization History

Year of Release – 1988

Company – Broderbund

Programmer - Ken Bull

Variations – 1 player

Fun Fact – The game was packaged with *Rand McNally's Concise Atlas of Europe*.

Where in Time is Carmen Sandiego?

Description – In this game you are once again a detective with ACME and you are in pursuit of Carmen Sandiego and her henchmen. This time you are chasing them throughout time, anywhere from 400 AD to 1950. You use travel throughout a time stream, use the clues to determine which place in time the thieves are hiding, obtain a warrant, and send out a Capture Robot to arrest them.

Educational Focus – US History, World History

Year of Release – 1989

Company – Broderbund

Programmer - Rodney Nelson

Variations – 1 player

Fun Fact – This game was packed with *The New America Desk Encyclopedia*.

Note – The Carmen Sandiego Series will be continued in the next book.

Logo Writer

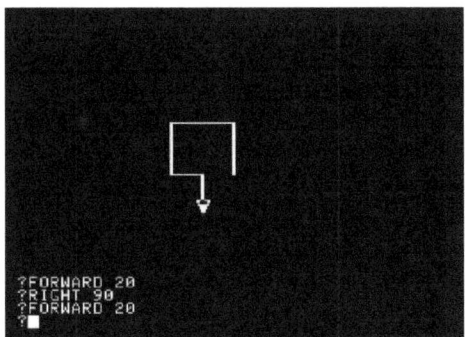

Description – *Logo* was a programming language that was created in 1967. With this program you can make shapes, miniature cartoons, games, and music videos. Your cursor was actually a turtle, who had a pencil attached to his rear. He made lines and designs based on directions that you give him. When I was in middle school, it was part of the computer class curriculum that we learn Logo. It was a lot of fun, but also lots of work. But like any project, it was nice to see the end result after you completed it.

I spoke briefly of a *Logo* related game in my previous book, the program called *Telly Turtle* for Colecovision. That was kind of *Logo-Light*, I suppose. But this is the full-on *Logo*. It was released for several other computers, but the Apple II/e version is by far the most superior, in my opinion anyway.

If you're going to give this a try, or if you mastered it in your younger days, I do recommend getting the instruction manual or looking for some of the old textbooks that were used in the late 80's. You can find them online, but just to warn you, the book is very long!

Educational Focus – Programming

Year of Release – 1982

Company - Logo Computer Systems, Inc. (LCSI)

Programmers – Wally Feurzeig, Seymour Papert & Cynthia Solomon

Variations – 1 player

Fun Fact – When the language was first created, they used an actual robot turtle to demonstrate the program.

Sesame Street

Since the early 70's, *Sesame Street* has been helping children learn and have fun while doing it.

It made sense that those great characters like Big Bird, Bert, Ernie and eventually Elmo would enter the world of edutainment gaming.

There would be several other games to be released over the years for various computers and gaming systems, but I'm going to talk about the ones that were released by Apple for the II/e computer.

Mix and Match

Description – This Sesame Street game has several mini-games to help young children (Preschool/Toddler) learn while having fun doing it.

Educational Focus – Memory, Physics, Spelling, Word Recognition

Year – 1982

Company – Apple Computer/Children's Television Workshop

Programmer – Unknown

Variations –

- 1 player

- *Mix and Match* – Create your own mixed-up Muppets.

- *Animal* - a memory game where the CPU tries to guess an animal when given clues by the player.

- *Layer Cake* - a puzzle game involving moving different cake layers between three platters but try not to get any crushed.

- *Raise the Flags* - a take on hangman where you get several guesses at figuring out the secret word.

Fun Fact – This was the second *Sesame Street*-themed game to be exclusively made for the Apple II/e.

Ernie's Quiz

Description – This game, made exclusively for Apple II/e contains three different mini games for Preschool and Toddler aged learners.

Educational Focus – Math, Memory, Creativity

Year of Release – 1981

Company – Apple Computers/Children's Television Workshop

Programmer – Unknown

Variations - 1 player

- *Face-It*: the player creates their own Muppet face.

- *Guess Who*: the player must guess a character's name as their picture is revealed.

- *Jelly Beans*: the player must correctly count the jellybeans in a jar.

Fun Fact – This was the first *Sesame Street* game made exclusively for the Apple II/e.

Ernie's Magic Shapes

Description - With the wave of his magic wand, Ernie the Magician makes a shape float over his head. Another wave, and a second shape appears on a table nearby. The player now decides whether or not the two shapes match. If so, and the player agrees, Ernie nods and the two shapes float together before disappearing. If not, Ernie shakes his head "no", waves his wand, and a new shape appears on the table.

Ernie's Magic Shapes has six levels of play. At the lower levels, the player compares one shape to another or the colors of two similar shapes. Levels four and five require greater visual discrimination since the target object is made up of several shapes and each one has to be matched individually. At the highest level, there is a complex mixture of both shapes and colors.[7]

Educational Focus – Shapes, Color Identification

Year of Release – 1987

Company – Hi-Tech Expressions/CTW Software Group

Programmer – Unknown

Variations –

- 1 Player

---

[7] https://www.myabandonware.com/game/ernie-s-magic-shapes-bqt#Apple%20II

- *Instructions*

- *Presto Shape-o*

- *Abracadabra…Colors!*

- *Zip Zap the Shapes*

- *Poof Pop the Colors*

- *Shazam! More Shapes*

- *Ta Dah! What a Figure*

Fun Fact – This would be the last game where Ernie was the main character.

Commodore 64

This computer took the world by storm, at times outselling all its competitors. I knew many people who had one of these while I was growing up in the 80's. All of them look back on the C64 fondly.

Sadly, one of the biggest problems with the C64 was that it was seen as mostly a gaming computer, which was not true. It had many of the same programs (like word processors, etc.) that other computers did. That was actually part of the reason that my own parents refused to get us a C64.

True, it did have a large selection of games, but there were some great edutainment games as well. Many of the game companies that I listed in previous chapters also released versions of their titles for the C64. So, for this chapter I'm going to discuss just a few games that I haven't covered yet. Yes, there are many more, but these ones I feel stand out amongst the others.

A good emulator to use is Hoxs64. You can find out more about it at this site:

https://www.hoxs64.net/

So, for those of you that actually know what *Load "*",8,1* means, this section is for you!

Romper Room's I Love My Alphabet

Description – Any kid that grew up in the 50's to the early 90's remembers *Romper Room*. It was a live-action, kid's show that simulated a preschool classroom. It had cool characters, puppets, a sweet teacher, students, and all kinds of things. It was a nice, safe place to learn. If only my real early educational experiences were like that! This game, like the show itself, is focused on early learning for preschoolers and toddlers. You have a character named Max, who looks like a tomato with legs, to help you along.

Educational Focus – Spelling, Word Recognition, Letter Recognition, Early Reading

Year of Release – 1984

Company – Five Star Software, Inc.

Programmers – Fred Tedsen and Lauren Elliott

Variations –

- *Watch the letters* which is a passive introduction to the letters in the alphabet. The player simply looks on as Max introduces each of the letters. For each letter Max will do an act (for example dance on d) which is then described with a simple sentence.

- *Press a letter* allows the player to press a letter on the keyboard and Max will then act out that letter.

- *Find the letter* has Max selecting a letter and the player then has to press the correct key on the keyboard. If the right one is picked Max will act out the letter.

- *Letter Quiz* has Max doing one of his acts and the player will then have to recognize it and enter the corresponding letter.[8]

Fun Fact – Most of the episodes of the show are lost because of the high cost of videotape and the fact that they recorded so many episodes. Some celebrities appeared as one of the children on the show, including Leonardo DiCaprio in 1979.

---

[8] https://www.mobygames.com/game/79072/romper-rooms-i-love-my-alphabet/

Number Nabber/Shape Grabber

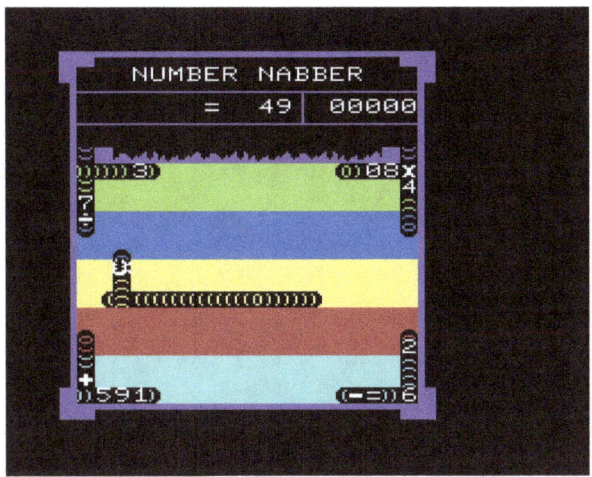

Description - The player controls a small character with a long prehensile tongue that burrows about underground trying to grab numbers or shapes. The goal is to complete mathematical formulas or create similar shapes as shown at the top of the screen. Each number, shape, or operation caught is individually placed in a slot at the top of the screen. Once the two sides balance, the player eats an 'equals' sign to complete the problem. A small monster moves about the screen that will send the player back to the center of the screen if it catches the player.[9]

Educational Focus – Math & Logic

Year – 1983

Company – Commodore Business Machines, Inc.

Programmer – Unknown

Variations – 4 levels of difficulty for both games

---

[9] https://www.mobygames.com/game/191933/number-nabber-shape-grabber/

Fun Fact – This game was originally released for the Commodore VIC-20 computer, which was the first computer Commodore released.

Sea Speller

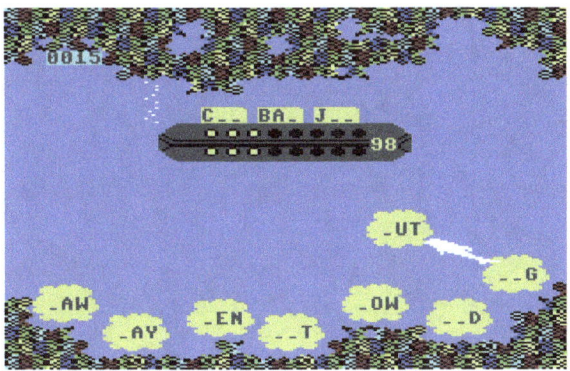

Description - In *Sea Speller* the player controls a dolphin whose task is to help a submarine reach the ocean floor before it runs out of air. This is done by picking up "letter sponges" scattered along the bottom of the sea and matching them with the signs on the sub's billboard to create words. Every complete word fires up another light on the submarine, and once they're all lit up, it descends to deeper waters for the next level - which ups the difficulty with longer words.

The quicker you are, the higher the score - if the sub reaches the bottom with air left over, a bonus is awarded; you can save time by using a single letter combination to create more than one word. Certain "magic words" (all related to the sea) will automatically send you to the next level to really speed things along.[10]

Educational Focus – Reading, Word Recognition

Year of Release – 1984

Company – Fisher Price Learning Software/Spinnaker Software Corporation

Programmer – Paul Munsey

Variations – 1 & 2 Player

---

[10] https://www.mobygames.com/game/65123/sea-speller/

Fun Fact – Fisher Price, like many other companies in the 80's, tried to get into the lucrative video game market, but weren't successful.

Elementary Math/Bingo Math

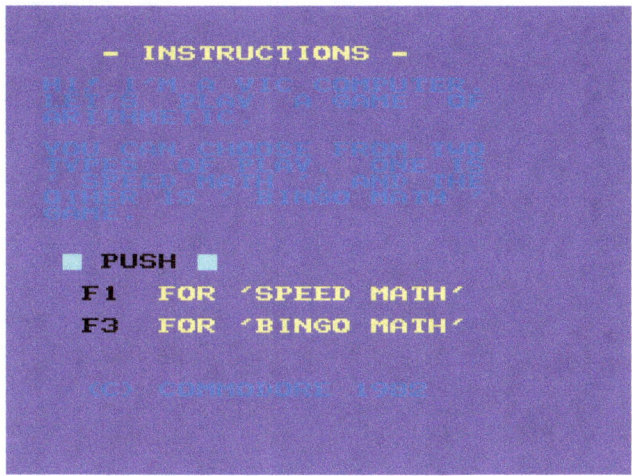

Description - *Elementary Math / Bingo Math* is a collection of two educational math games. The game helps improve skills in addition, subtraction, multiplication and division. Points are awarded based on speed and math problems get harder the higher the current score.[11]

Educational Focus – Basic Math (Addition, Subtraction, Multiplication & Division)

Year – 1982

Company – Bally Manufacturing Company/ Commodore Business Machines, Inc.

Programmer – Unknown

Variations – 4 – per order of operation selected. Difficulty adjusts automatically for player's skill.

Fun Fact – This game was originally released in 1978 for the short-lived Bally Astrocade.

---

[11] https://www.mobygames.com/game/165759/elementary-math-bingo-math/

States and Capitols Tutorial

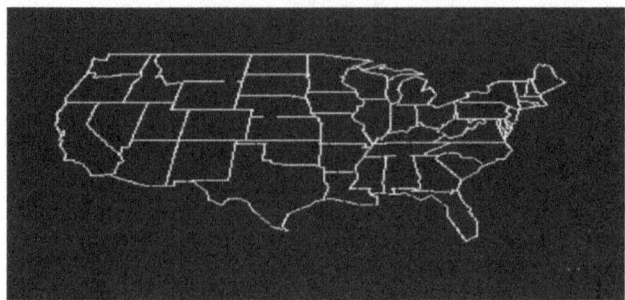

Description – In this, seemingly indie game, you are given a map of the United States and a particular State is highlighted. The player then must give the correct name of that State and then its Capital. It's a simple game, but one that is very well made, and I highly recommend it to learners of all ages.

Educational Focus – Social Studies

Year of Release – 1984

Company – S.M. Thorpe Co.

Programmer – S.M. Thorpe

Variations – 1 Player

Fun Fact – Indie games were and still are much more common for home computers. Back in the day, games and programs were traded around from person to person, and there was no telling how many games were actually made and released to the general public. That is part of the reason why getting an accurate count of how many games were made for a computer is difficult, if not impossible.

Math Blaster

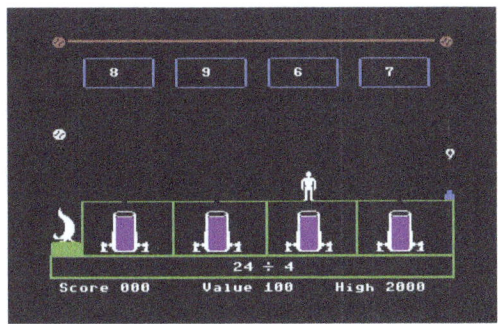

Description – The company's motto was *Educational Software that Works*! I have to agree as this edutainment game is focused on math skills for grades 1-6. The player uses the cannon to shoot at the correct answer to the given problem. Parents and teachers can also add their own questions for students.

Educational Focus – Math for grades 1-6 (Addition, Subtraction, Multiplication, Division, Fractions, Decimals, and Percentages)

Year – 1985

Company – Davidson & Associates Inc.

Programmer – Richard K. Eckert, Jr.

Variations –

- *1 player*
- *Addition*
- *Subtraction*
- *Multiplication*
- *Division*
- *Fractions & Decimals*

- *Data Disk*

Fun Fact – The math programs aren't randomly generated; they are in pre-programmed sets.

MS DOS

For those of us whose parents purchased a PC, we thank you. But for those whose parents didn't, I'll explain what MS-DOS was. It stood for Microsoft Disk Operating System. All computers that were either IBM or IBM compatibles ran on MS-DOS until the advent of Windows.

In the early days of PC's, you would usually put the DOS disk in the floppy drive before you started the computer up. As I said in my last book, hard drives weren't used for storage back then. Then, when the prompt came up, you would take out the DOS disk and put in your program (game) disk. Unless you knew the name of the exe or com file, you would type in *dir/w* (always put in the /w because if you don't, you'll get a long list). Then you would look for the exe or com file and you would type it in, and the program would start up.

That was PC computing back in the day. Things changed when all PCs were equipped with Windows. Then it was point and click.

Nowadays, the only time people work with DOS is when they want to play old school games (like the ones that I'm going to list). A really cool emulator to play these and many other DOS games is DOSBox. You can find instructions on how to use it at this link: https://www.dosbox.com/

So, for all of us who got to know the ins and outs of exe, bat or com files and what they did and didn't do, this next section is for you guys.

Reader Rabbit

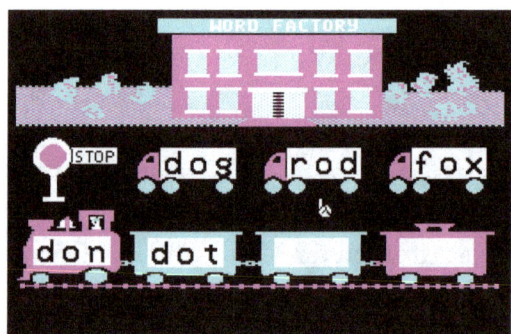

Description – This game helps with phonics and reading skills and it is geared towards learners ages 3 to 7.

Educational Focus – Reading, Spelling, Word Recognition

Year of Release – 1987

Company – The Learning Company

Programmer – Leslie Grimm

Variations –

- *Word Sorter*

- *Picture Labeler*

- *Word Train*

- *Word Memory*

Fun Fact – This would be the first game in a long-running, edutainment series.

Rocky's Boots

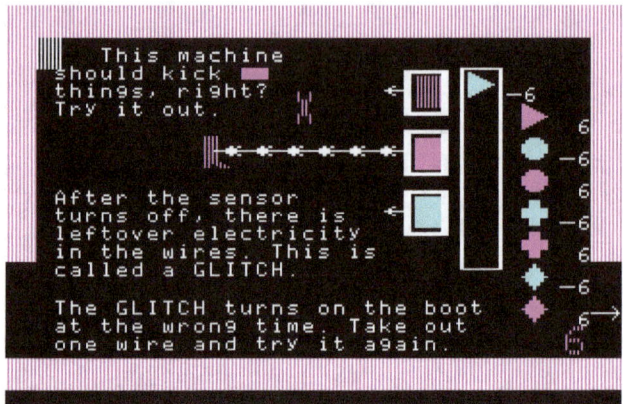

Description - You control a nondescript square, moving it about several rooms. Each room contains basic electronic parts like AND, OR and NOT gates, flip-flops, delays and clocks. You can pick these up and combine them to build simple or complex circuits.

After a helpful tutorial, the task in the game is to build "kicking" machines: Objects of different colors move through an area and turn sensor outputs on and off. You now have to build a circuit that activates a kicking device which kicks the right objects out. When you do it just right, Rocky the raccoon dances a little jig to a joyful melody for you!

The game also features an editor where you can build your very own kicking puzzle.[12]

Educational Focus – Logic, Computer Circuitry

Year of Release – 1984

Company – The Learning Company

Programmer – Warren Robinett and Leslie Grimm

Variations –

- *How to Move*

---

[12] https://www.mobygames.com/game/42318/rockys-boots/

- *Building Machines*

- *Logic Gates*

- *Rocky's Boots*

- *Flipflops*

- *Rocky's Challenge*

Fun Fact – *Rocky's Boots* won several awards and is still held in high esteem by both parents and programmers.

Number Muncher

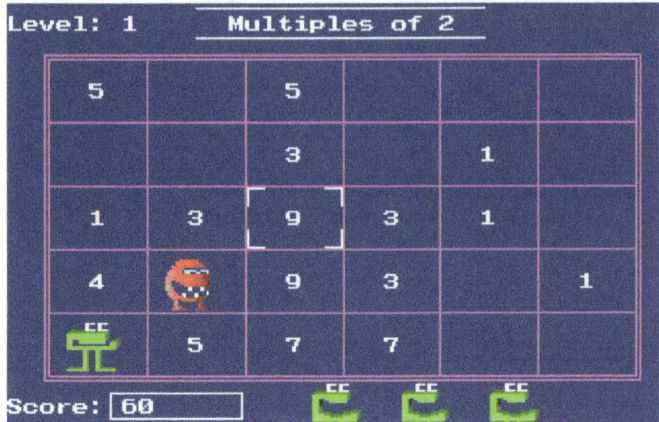

Description – A later release from MECC, the company that made many great edutainment titles for the Apple II/e in the 80's. In this game you use your Muncher to eat numbers to solve math problems of several different varieties. If you can eat enough numbers and not get eaten yourself by the Troggles, you will join The Muncher Hall of Fame.

Educational Focus – Math Application & Math Reasoning

Year of Release – 1990

Company – MECC

Programmer – R. Philip Bouchard

Variations –

- *Multiples*

- *Factors*

- *Primes*

- *Equality*

- *Inequality*

Fun Fact – *PC Magazine* called it one of the Top 10 Best Educational PC Games of the 80's.[13]

---

[13] https://www.pcmag.com/news/10-educational-pc-games-every-80s-kid-loved

Word Munchers

Description - The player moves his muncher creature on a board, the task is to eat the right words with the same vowel sound as a word shown at the top of the screen. Sometimes, unfriendly creatures called Troggles enter the playfield. They come in different types with different patterns and abilities, and running into them depletes Muncher lives, as does eating incorrect words. Occasionally, safety squares appear which offer some temporary protection. It's possible to make some adjustments to the game, such as the difficulty by using the management options.[14]

Educational Focus – Vowel Sounds, Pronunciation

Year of Release – 1990

Company – MECC

Programmer – R. Philip Bouchard

Variations – Various Levels of Difficulty and hundreds of game board variations.

Fun Fact – MECC was so confident that parents and students would enjoy this game, that it had a 30-day money-back guarantee.

---

[14] https://www.mobygames.com/game/71170/word-munchers/

Donald's Alphabet Chase

Description - *Donald's Alphabet Chase* is an educational game for children ages 2-5 featuring Donald Duck. Donald's alphabet letters have escaped and are now hiding throughout the house! You need to help Donald locate all 26 of the letters and put them back in place. By pressing a letter on the keyboard, an animation is displayed where Donald finds and catches that letter. There are six different screens a letter may be hiding on, and each letter features a different animation. When all of the letters have been collected, the game is over, and a bonus screen is displayed.[15]

Educational Focus – Letter Recognition

Year of Release – 1988

Company – Disney Software

Programmers – Ethan Grimes, George Ghali, & Lee Whitney

Variations – 1 Player

Fun Fact – Donald Duck would go on to be the star of many video games, on both game consoles and computers.

---

[15] https://www.mobygames.com/game/15038/donalds-alphabet-chase/

TRS-80 Color Computer

Let me start this chapter off by saying that I didn't have any real exposure to this computer when

I was growing up. One teacher at the middle school that I went to, had a TRS-80 in his

classroom, but he only allowed the students in the higher classes to use it. Back then, students

were tracked and those that were seen as advanced students got more privileges than those who

weren't. I was one of those who weren't, so I didn't get to use that computer. But from what I

remember, it was outdated, even for 1987. It ran on cassettes, and at that point, at least on this

side of the pond, we used floppy disks. Other than just watching someone else play on it and

getting a few glances, which was about all I knew about that type of computer.

Fast forward many years, and while I was doing research for my YouTube channel, I learned

more about the TRS-80, affectionately known as the *Co-Co* by its loyal fanbase, short for Color

Computer. I didn't realize there were so many dedicated users. Back in my day, all my friends who owned computers had either a PC of some kind or a C64. That was about it. Our schools had Apple II's and occasionally some rebel teacher would purchase a Tandy (PC-compatible) for their own use, but that was about it. Even though my father was a frequent visitor to Radio Shack, the home of the TRS-80 (which stood for Tandy Radio Shack, by the way), I don't think it ever crossed his mind to get this little microcomputer. By the time we were in the market for our own home computer, in the early 90's, Radio Shack was pushing hard to sell its Tandy Computer.

The Tandy Corporation would start making computers way back in 1977 and the final one of the TRS-80's called the Model 4 would come out in 1991. After that, they would focus on PC compatible computers until discontinuing their own line totally in the mid-90's. After that Radio Shack would sell computers by other manufacturers until their eventual closing.

The Co-Co's were pretty easy to use, as it took commands in BASIC. I was able to acquire an emulator called the VCC (Virtual Color Computer). Like the Co-Co itself, it's not too difficult to figure out, though I would recommend watching a tutorial on using it, if you didn't grow up using an actual Co-Co. This guy has a great video and shows you how to get it running: https://youtu.be/RD1cexRPpT4 and tells you great places to find different pieces of software and connect with other fans of the Co-Co. You can get the VCC here: http://imacoconut.com/

So, for those who thought that floppy disks were new-fangled-cityfied-inventions and thought that Windows was something that you put in your house, this is for you. Many thanks to Steve Strow for his assistance and guidance.

Bumble Games

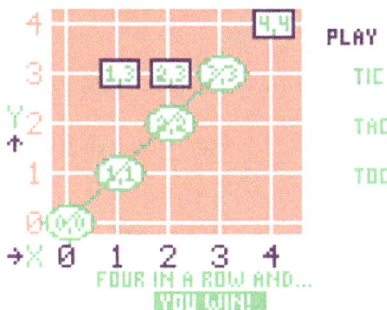

Description – This game is geared towards young learners aged 4-10. There are six different games to choose from.

Educational Focus – Graphing, Math, Logic

Year of Release – 1982

Company – The Learning Company

Programmer – Leslie Grimm

Variations – One to Two Players

- *Find Your Number* - Bumble will think of a secret number between 1 and 5. You need to guess it! After each incorrect guess, a clue will appear on the screen indicating whether your guess was too high or too low.

- *Find the Bumble* - Bumble is hiding somewhere in a 4x4 grid, and you need to find him! By entering in coordinates, you can guess a grid location to see if he's there. If not, a clue will be displayed indicating in what direction he is hiding.

- *Butterfly Hunt* - Bumble's butterfly is lost, and you need to help find it! To search, you once again need to enter in grid coordinates, this time in a 5x5 grid. If your guess is unsuccessful, a clue will be displayed indicating in what direction the butterfly is hiding.

- *Visit from Space* - Bumble's cousin is visiting from space! You need to find out where he is by searching a 5x5 grid. You can examine a part of the grid by entering in its coordinates; if your guess is incorrect, a clue will be displayed in what direction Bumble's cousin is hiding.

- *Tic Tac Toc* - This is a variation of tic tac toe and is for two players only. Given a 5x5 grid, each player takes turns placing X's and O's on the grid. Four X's or four O's in a row (in any direction) will win the game.

- *Bumble Dots* - This is a drawing game. Given an 11x11 grid, you can select different coordinates on the grid and draw lines between them. Several pictures are included with the game which provide clues as to where you should draw lines, or you can create your own pictures from scratch. You can optionally have the game color in your picture when it's done.

Fun Fact – There would be two games in the Bumble series. This was the first game.

Bumble Plot

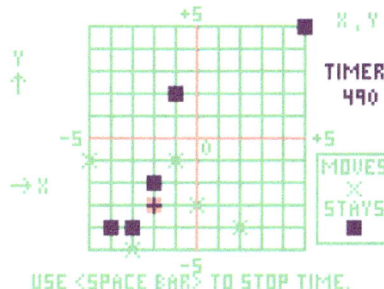

Description - Bumble *Plot* is made up of five increasingly challenging games to help children develop geometry skills. For children aged 8-13.

Educational Focus – Geometry

Year of Release – 1982

Company – The Learning Company

Programmer – Leslie Grimm

Variations – 1 to 2 Players

- *Trap & Guess*

- *Bumblebug*

- *Hidden Treasure*

- *Bumble Art*

- *Roadblock*

Fun Fact – While doing research for the books in this series, I found very few games that focus on geometry, surprisingly.

Easy Reader – Learn About Sounds

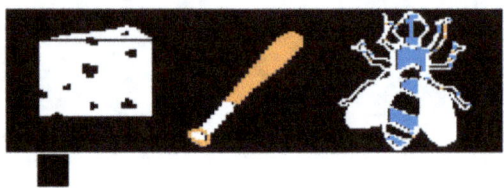

```
CHEESE BAT BEE
```

```
GOAL=6 RIGHT IN A ROW-YOU HAVE 0
IF YOU HEAR THE 'B' SOUND AS IN
BOX, PRESS THE 'B' KEY.  IF YOU
DON'T, PRESS THE '/' SLASH KEY.
```

Description – *Easy Reader* assists young learners with learning to read by introducing letter sounds.

Educational Focus – Reading

Year of Release – 1983

Company – American Educational Computer

Programmer – Unknown

Variations –

- *Initial Consonants – B, C, D*

- *Initial Consonants – F, G, H*

- *Initial Consonants – J, K, L*

- *Initial Consonants – M, N, P*

- *Initial Consonants – Q, R, S*

- *Initial Consonants – T, V, W*

- *Initial Consonants – Y*

- *Initial Consonants – Z*

- *Short Vowels – A*

- *Short Vowels – E*

- *Short Vowels – I*

- *Short Vowels – O*

- *Short Vowels – U*

Fun Fact – I couldn't find anything online about the company that made this game, so I am assuming it was a one-time product. Regardless, this one product is well made.

Math Invaders

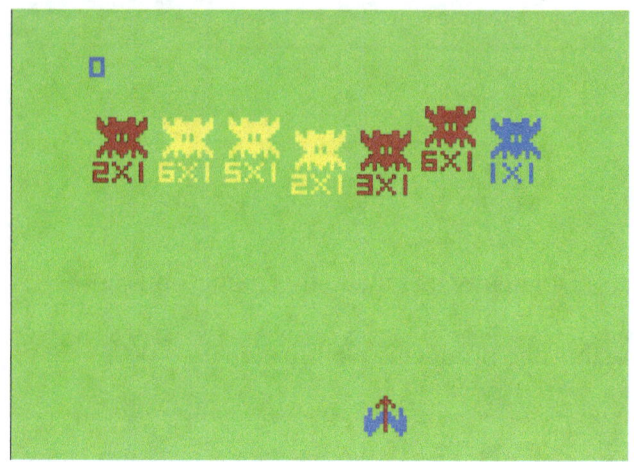

Description – Aliens are coming, and you are earth's only defense! Unlike *Space Invaders*, you can't simply shoot down the aliens. You have to solve math problems and then shoot the alien whose math problem matches your answer. You have to act fast, or the aliens will zap you and the earth!

Educational Focus – Math

Year of Release – 1983

Company – Pyramid Software (Australia)

Programmer – Dean Hodgson

Variations – Skill Level 0-10

Fun Fact – This game is an educational twist on *Space Invaders*, a very popular arcade game from that time period.

Spelling

```
SAY THESE WORDS
WALL
BALL
CALL
SMALL
TALL
MALL
PRESS ENTER
```

Description – This game helps learners with their spelling and memorization. There are various levels of difficulty to accommodate learners of all ages. A list of words is given, and then students are given each word quickly and then will type back the word they saw. As time goes on the words increase in difficulty.

Educational Focus – Reading, Word Recognition

Year of Release – 1983?

Company – Pyramid Software

Programmer – Unknown

Variations – 1 to 200 difficulty levels

Fun Fact – Not much credit is given to whomever created this game, other than the company who distributed it. This is an example of a game where less is sufficient.

ZX Spectrum

To most gamers on this side of the Atlantic Ocean, the ZX Spectrum is pretty much an unknown

computer. We and our brother and sister gamers in the UK did share our love of the C64, but the

ZX Spectrum (or Specky as they call it), was something that they got to keep to themselves.

I wouldn't have even heard of this computer if it weren't for another YouTube channel that I

watched called Kim Justice (much love and admiration). And I'm the type of person that if I

hear about a vintage gaming console or computer, I have to try it out. No matter what.

When I first tried out the Spectrum, thanks to an emulator, I have to say that I was impressed.

Yes, the variety of colors is quite limiting, but don't forget that I started computer gaming back

in the days of CGA graphics, so it's not an issue for me. What I really did like best of all was the

smoothness and response from controls, that sometimes-plagued vintage PC's. I was also impressed with the huge number of games that the Spectrum had, many of them exclusive to the UK. And, no, they weren't all soccer games. A lot of them were, but not all of them.

Along with its huge library of games, there were also programs, and of course, edutainment games. I'm going to discuss a few, as there are many out there.

So, for those of you that see absolutely nothing wrong with playing both your computer games and your music on cassette, and those that actually understand the rules of cricket, this is for you!

Jungle Maths

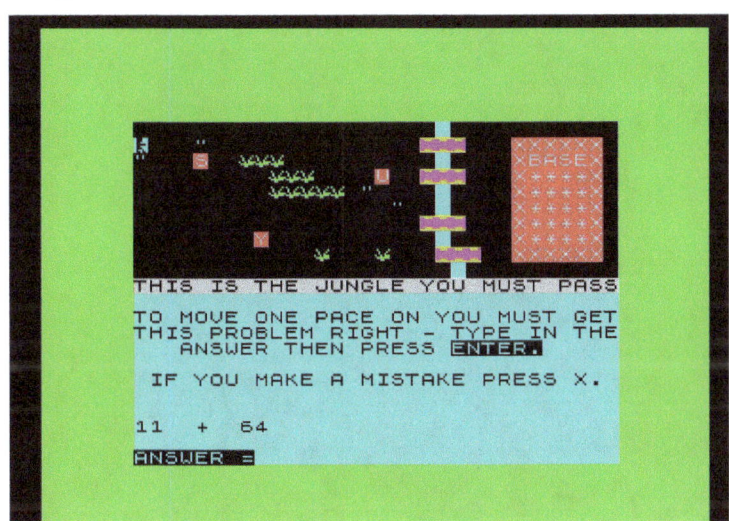

Description – In this game you take on the role of an explorer deep in the jungle. You have to answer math questions in order to get around. If you miss a question you fall into a deep hole and die. You only have five lives; can you make it?

Educational Focus – Math

Year of Release – 1982

Company – Scisoft

Programmer – Unknown

Variations –

- *Addition/Subtraction*

- *Positive/Negative Numbers*

- *Number of Digits in the Questions*

- *Figure sizes: 10, 100, or 1,000*

- *Answers are positive or negative*

- *Decimals or not*

- Time limit

Fun Fact – In the UK they call the subject maths not math. This is because math is short for mathematics, and they feel that adding the s on the end is a more appropriate abbreviation.

Biology Intro.

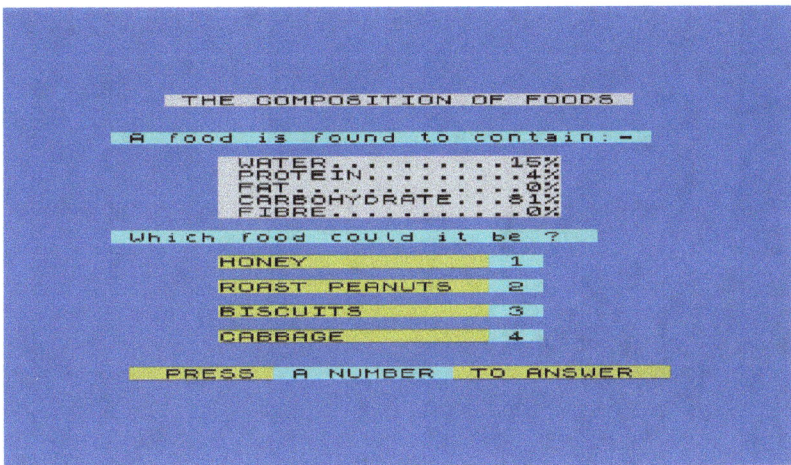

Description – This text game asks you a series of multiple-choice questions about different Biology topics. If you get a question wrong, it will explain to you why the answer was incorrect and will give you more than one chance to pick the correct answer.

Educational Focus – Biology

Year of Release – 1984

Company – Longman Software

Programmer – Unknown

Variations –

- *Composition of Foods*

- *Vitamins and Minerals*

- *Daily Energy Needs*

Fun Fact – This was the first in a series of Biology, text-based games from Longman Software.

Fun to Learn – Geography

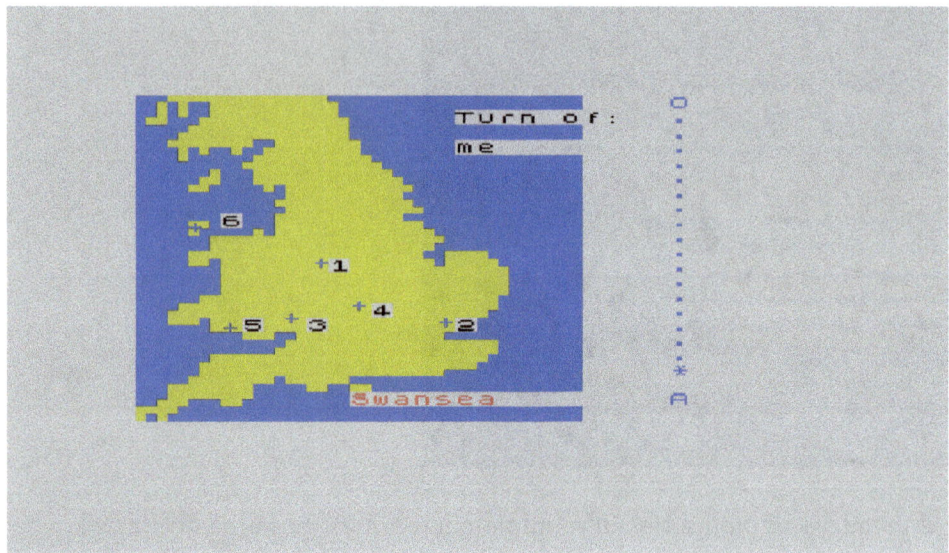

Description – In this game you and up to three of your classmates will race to a prescribed destination. You are given a map of England and Wales, and your job is correctly pinpoint the locations of certain towns on the map. The first to make it to the destination is the winner.

Educational Focus – Geography of England and Wales

Year of Release – 1982

Company – Sinclair Research

Programmer – Unknown

Variations – 1 to 4 players

Fun Fact – From playing this game, you either must live in the UK or be very familiar with it as many of the towns listed were ones that I'd never heard of!

Learning to Read Music

Description – You are given either the treble or the bass clef and it is your job to identify specific notes. You must press the correct key on the piano that corresponds with the note that was played.

Education Focus – Reading Music, Piano

Year of Release – 1984

Company – Rose Software

Programmer – Unknown

Variations – One Player

Fun Fact – I highly recommend this game to any person who is starting out learning the piano. It will be a valuable resource for any music, choir, or band class.

Learn to Read 1

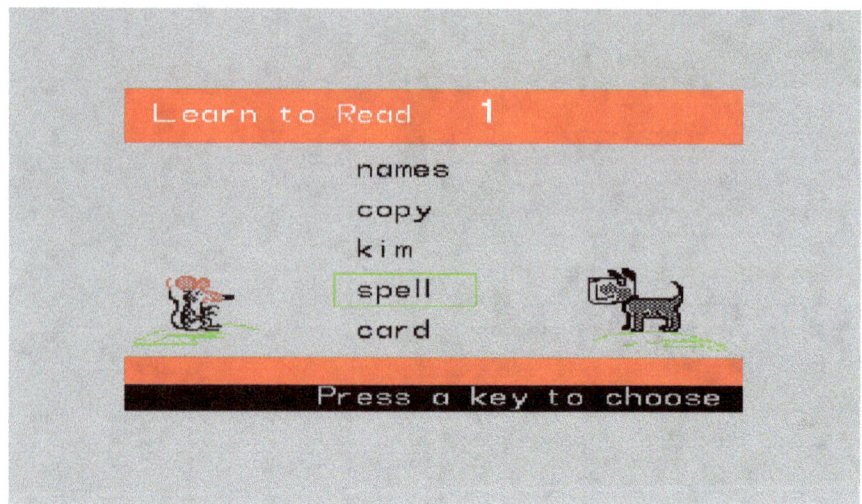

Description – This edutainment game, the first in a series, is geared towards young readers. The activities help learners to associate words with pictures, reinforce memorization, and make reading enjoyable.

Educational Focus – Reading

Year of Release – 1984

Company – MacMillan Software/Sinclair Research

Programmer – Unknown

Variations –

- *Name* – match the picture to its corresponding word

- *Copy* – retype the name of the animal

- *Kim* – the animal's name is briefly shown on screen, then the learner types it back from memory

- *Spell* – The learner is given pictures with their corresponding words. After the picture goes away the learner must write the word to describe the animal, whether its name or what it is.

- *Card* – the learner must find matching pictures under the cards (Memory)

Fun Fact – This was the first in a series of edutainment games. As the games progress, the words get more challenging.

What's the Time - Hours

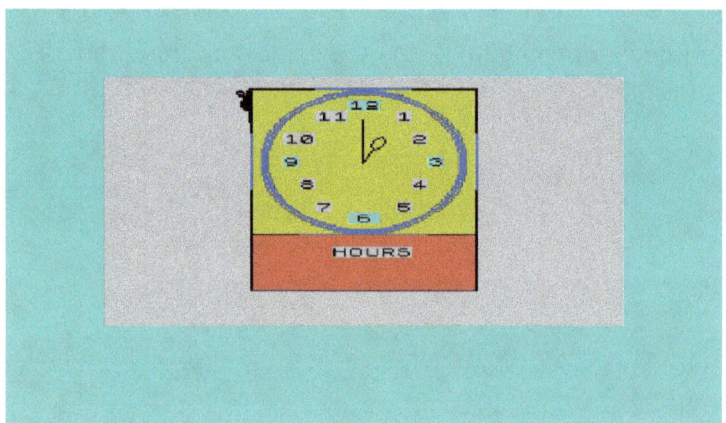

Description – The goal is for the learner to be able to read an analog clock, which as a teacher, I am saddened by the large number of students who cannot read one. I guess that has been taken out of the curriculum?! Anyway, this game teaches the learners to use associations in order to remember the correct placement of the hands for a specific hour (examples – 8:00 the time I get up and 9:00 the time I go to work). This game is a must for young learners, of course, but also for those who never learned to read an analog clock.

Educational Focus – Telling time on an analog clock

Year of Release – 1983

Company – Collins Educational

Programmer – Unknown

Variations – 1 player

Fun Fact – This first game in the series focuses on hours, and the subsequent games are about half hours and quarter hours.

Amstrad CPC

And last of all we have the Amstrad CPC (Colour Personal Computer). This 8 bit computer system was released in 1984 and was discontinued in 1990. During its life it was seen mostly as a gaming computer, which unlike the C64 was a reputation well earned. It was never released in North America, but had a following in the UK, Spain, France, and other German-speaking countries of Europe.

This was another computer that I hadn't heard of until I started to watch Kim Justice's YouTube channel, as it was relatively unknown in the US. I'm not a big fan of the computer. It kind of reminded me a lot of a DOS computer with VGA graphics. This fact and other hardware issues didn't help it stand out from the competition: C64 and ZX Spectrum, which had a pretty strong hold on consumers in Europe.

In my AVP Arcade vs Port videos on my channel, I do focus the CPC versions of established games and critique them compared to ports that were made for more established computers and consoles. Until recently, I hadn't heard of any educational games at all for this computer. I was only able to find one series of games, which I will discuss here.

I'm not at all surprised that the CPC didn't last. The other computers around that time had games, of course, but they had other software that would make purchasing them more practical. Just having nice graphics and some well-known games isn't enough to keep a computer relevant in such a competitive market.

Fun School Series

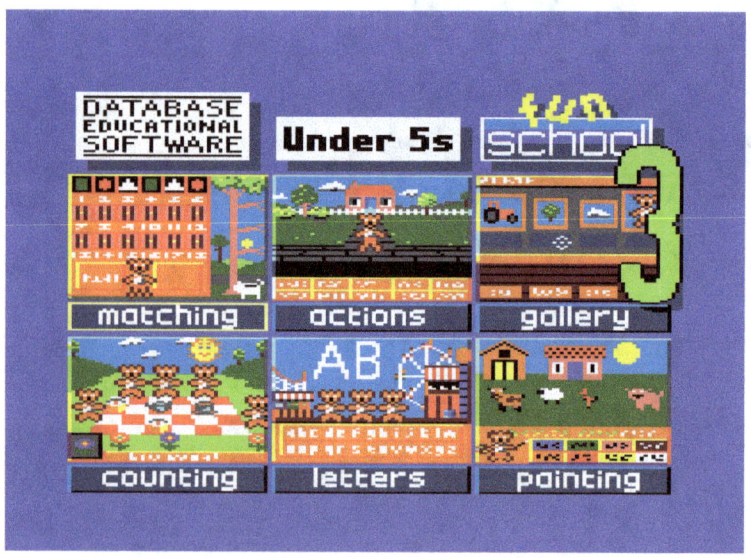

Description - These six small educational games star Freddy the Frog. Each uses simple controls to ensure that children can play without difficulty from the software.

Using forward, back, left and right keys Freddy must get to various important buildings as depicted on the screen. In Adding he is presented with a network of lily pads, some of which contain numbers or mathematical symbols. Land on these in the correct order to produce a correct sum. In the Toyshop, first identify toys from their names, then choose a toy at a specified price, and then combine goods to meet a specified price limit.

Electricity allows you to learn about circuits - by working out whether an existing layout will work, and modifying it so that it will. The next game involves telling the time, so as to get the prince his key. Funtext teaches information searching using a Ceefax-type environment.[16]

Educational Focus – Time, Money, Basic Math, Early Reading, Electricity

Year of Release – 1990

Company – Database Educational Software

Programmers – Darrell Ithell, Bob Hamilton, William Cochrane

Variations –

- *Collect*

- *Toyshop*

- *Funtext*

- *Journey*

- *Time*

- *Electricity*

Fun Fact – There were six games in this series, and they would get a wide release on all the computers of the day.

---

[16] https://www.mobygames.com/game/24379/fun-school-3-for-5-to-7-year-olds/

Epilogue

So that does it for this edition of *A Guide to Edutainment Gaming*. There are several other games for each computer that I mentioned, and many of the games listed were made for multiple computers, as well. I wanted to just focus on the games that I personally have played or used in my classroom. If there are other titles that you feel should have been included in this book, I might just make a follow-up to this specific time period. Drop me a line and let me know what you think.

Before the hate mail starts, I'm going to address why there wasn't a section on the Atari 8 computers. In my research I found that many edutainment game companies didn't make their titles for the Atari 8. I'm not sure why this was, I suspect it was something political. Later, some titles were made for the Atari ST, but that will be the subject of another book. When it came to games, the Atari 8 had them, but when it came to edutainment software, it was lacking, somewhat. Many of the *Sesame Street* titles that I mentioned in the first book that were intended for the Atari 5200 did make it to the Atari 8. It happens sometimes that software companies do pick and choose where they want to port their software to. I remember when I was young and would go to a computer store with my family. You would see rows and rows of games and other types of software for PC, but probably only one shelf dedicated to Mac. Somehow Apple did hold on, and with some great innovations like the I-Pod and I-Pad they have managed to stay in business. The same can't be said for some of the computers that I talked about in this book. Young people today didn't grow up during the time period when parents had to choose from multiple computer formats like when I was young. Now it's either a PC or a Mac, for the most part. There are some who swear by both. I've always been a PC person and I don't see me changing anytime soon. My wife gave me an I-Mac not too long ago, and I have to tell you that I was impressed with both its speed and efficiency. I plan to learn more about it. Young people today only hear about the Co-Co or the Commodore 64 from older relatives or if they happen on a site like Amazon and see the plug-and-play versions of vintage consoles or computers. Software itself has changed, as consumers can download a program rather than having to purchase one on a CD. The same applies to game consoles as well.

Technology changes so rapidly that it's hard to keep up sometimes. However, one thing that won't change is the value of edutainment gaming. No matter how old or new the games are, they are always relevant. Learning never goes out of style, so why should the games that help our children to learn?

In my next book in this series, I will discuss edutainment games for the 8- and 16-bit consoles from the late 80's into the 90's. If you have any suggestions, please let me know. I'm always happy to hear from my viewers. You can find me on my social media platforms, or simply drop me an email @ anthonyventrello@gmail.com Also, please share some memories you have of any of the games listed in this book. I'd love to hear from you.

Other Works by Anthony E. Ventrello:

- *Bloody Kisses* written under the pen name Archie E. Ouglie

- *Straying from the Wrong Path*

- *Of Tears, Passion and Hope: A Poetry Collection*

- *Hope for Tomorrow, Lessons from Yesterday: A Poetry Collection*

- *The Haunted Carnival: An Emily and Louise Mystery* w/ JoAnna Ventrello

- *Bride of Blood – First Kiss*

- *The Willow Arboretum* w/ JoAnna Ventrello

- *Father Time and the Last of the Passenger Pigeons* w/ JoAnna Ventrello

- *Merrygold and the Minotaur* w/ JoAnna Ventrello

- *Behind the Waterfall* w/ JoAnna Ventrello

- *Greenlee's Big Day* w/ JoAnna Ventrello

- *Of Love, Lust and Romance: A Poetry Collection*

- *Why We Prefer Cats* (Deluxe Edition)

- *The Fart Encyclopedia*

- *The Willow Arboretum Anthology* w/JoAnna Ventrello

- *A Journey in Darkness: The Life and Music of the Man Called "IT"*

- *Above, Below and Beyond: A Poetry Anthology*

- *Love of a Lifetime* w/Anthony Hanson

- *The History of Gaming: According to a middle-aged guy who likes old video games and plays with puppets*

- *A Guide to Edutainment Gaming: The Early Console Years*

- *The Thing in the Attic and Other Stories*

- *The Tale of the Knight and the Princess*

For more information, please visit me at:
http://www.facebook.com/anthonyeventrello
http://anthonyventrello.wixsite.com/mysite
www.amazon.com/author/anthonyventrello
http://www.youtube.com/classicgamer74